BARRY BONDS

BARRY
RECORD BREAKER
BONDS

Jeff Savage

LERNER SPORTS

AN IMPRINT OF LERNER PUBLISHING GROUP

To Bob Gallicano, the biggest Giants fan I know

LernerSports
An imprint of Lerner Publishing Group
241 First Avenue North
Minneapolis, MN 55401 U.S.A.

Website address: www.lernerbooks.com

Library of Congress Cataloging-in Publication Data

Savage, Jeff, 1961–
    Barry Bonds : record breaker / by Jeff Savage.
        p.   cm.
    Summary: Presents a biography of the power hitter for the San Francisco Giants who in 2001 broke Mark McGwire's single-season home run record and earned his fourth Most Valuable Player award.
    ISBN: 0–8225–0472–3 (pbk. : alk. paper)
    1. Bonds, Barry, 1964– —Juvenile literature.   2. Baseball players—United States—Biography—Juvenile literature. [1. Bonds, Barry, 1964– 2. Baseball players. 3. African Americans—Biography.] I. Title.
GV865.63 S385 2002
796.357'092—dc21   2002000196

Manufactured in the United States of America
2 3 4 5 6 7 – JR – 08 07 06 05 04 03

Contents

1

The Home Run Zone

Barry Bonds started the 2001 season with a specific goal. He aimed to hit more home runs than he had the previous year (49). Why? Willie Mays told him that a player of Barry's caliber should be able to. So, to improve his game and to help his team, Barry choked up on his bat and kept practicing his swing. Throughout his career, Barry has committed himself to becoming the best player he can be. That pursuit would land him in the record books in 2001 as one of the best to ever play the game of baseball.

Barry got off to a great start. On April 17, he hit his 500th career home run, putting him in the record books among only a handful of elite players. "I never dreamed of hitting 500 home runs," Barry said. "Everything after that is like icing on the cake." By April's end, 11 homers iced that cake. People were already talking about Mark McGwire's 1998 record of 70 home runs in one season.

Reporters started to question Barry about his intentions. Never one for the media, he refused to fuel the hype. Barry insisted that winning was his main interest. "I don't want the home run record," Barry explained, "I want a [championship] ring." Whether he wanted it or not, Barry was slugging homers toward the record even faster than McGwire had in 1998.

Then Barry hit a dry spell before the All-Star break. He endured 63 plate appearances in 14 games without a home run. Reporters kept asking Barry what went wrong. Sometimes Barry seemed disappointed, but he had confidence in his ability. The zone returned. "Everything is perfect in that one particular second," Barry described. "It's in slow motion. You don't hear anything, you don't even feel it hit your bat. That's the zone."

Once the drought ended, Barry homered so often that other teams feared him. Eventually, pitchers stopped throwing strikes, and Barry started walking. He soon had more intentional walks in a season than any player in major league history. "You can't do anything if you're not pitched to," Barry said. "You take what they give you." Although frustrated, Barry didn't mind the walks that helped his team win.

With few good pitches to swing at, Barry still whacked home runs out of the ballpark with amazing frequency. "One of the things that makes what he's doing so amazing is that no one is really pitching to

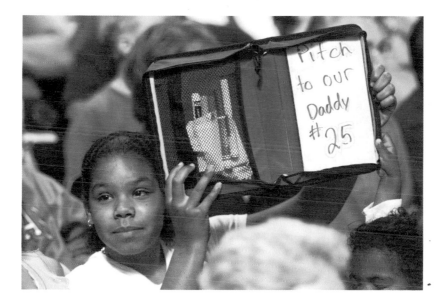

him," said Barry's friend and fellow player, Tony Gwynn. Even when they were too far behind to win, many teams intentionally walked Barry, but they still couldn't stop him.

Barry tucked number 69 under his belt anyway. He was just one away from tying McGwire's record, eight days before the end of the season. There were two teams yet to play. With the zone he was in, many fans believed that Barry would certainly achieve the new record. One concern worried Barry—the Dodgers!

The Giants were scheduled to play their notorious rivals last. Back in April, the Dodgers furiously complained when the Giants paused a game to celebrate Barry's 500th career home run. Would they give Barry

After hitting his 70th home run, Barry celebrated his achievement at home plate with the Giants and his son, the Giants' batboy.

any good pitches to hit? Barry hoped to get the job done against the Astros, before the Dodgers had a chance to snuff out his efforts.

The Astros would not cooperate. They pitched around Barry throughout the frustrating three-game series, throwing ball after ball. Disappointed, the home team crowd at the Astrodome booed each walk. They had come to witness Barry make history.

In the ninth inning of the last game of the series against the Astros, Barry slowly entered the batter's box. Pitcher Wilfredo Rodriguez eyed his competition from the mound. Playing in only his second major league game, the rookie was determined to strike out Barry. He wound up and hurled a fast ball. Strike one. Perhaps there was an opportunity after all. Barry carefully watched the next pitch—a familiar ball. Then, on the 1 1 count, Rodriguez fired a 93 mile-per-hour pitch across the plate. Barry smacked it, sending his 70th home run of the season 454 feet, straight into the record books alongside Mark McGwire.

Barry let go of his bat and lifted his arms in the air. The crowd jumped to its feet. As he trotted slowly around the bases, Barry reveled in the deserved adoration. His teammates rushed to congratulate him. At home plate, Barry hugged his son and pointed to his wife and daughters. He had accomplished his goal, and then some.

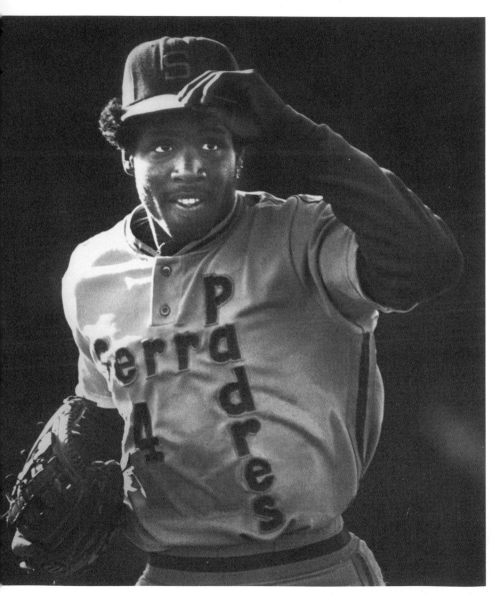

Barry was an outstanding athlete for Serra High School.

2

Bobby's Boy

Like most young boys, Barry Lamar Bonds dreamed of someday being a professional athlete. Unlike most boys, whose favorite sport changes from season to season, Barry knew all along what sport he wanted to play when he grew up—*baseball*. Barry had the team all figured out, too—the *Giants*.

Barry had good reasons for his choices. His father, Bobby Bonds, was a professional baseball player. The family lived in San Carlos, California, a short drive south of Candlestick Park, where the Giants played.

Bobby was 18 years old when Barry was born on July 24, 1964. A year later, Bobby signed with the Giants organization. Bobby hoped that someday his son would be a major leaguer, also.

Bobby was worried when his baby boy seemed to be lefthanded. Being a lefty would limit the positions Barry could play on a baseball team.

Bobby and Pat Bonds raised their children in California.

Nearly all second basemen, shortstops, and third basemen are righthanded because it's easier for right-handed players to throw to first base. A righthanded player throws the ball across his or her body to first. A lefthanded player must throw the ball away from his or her body to make that throw.

Bobby wanted Barry to be righthanded, and he wouldn't let his son take his baby bottle with his left hand. "I'd pull it away and get him to take it with his right," Bobby said. "But then he'd just switch it over." Barry was a lefty, and that was that. Bobby would just have to help Barry be the best lefthanded player he could be.

Bobby Bonds was an outstanding player for the Giants.

When Barry was two, he could hit a whiffle ball hard enough to break a window. When he was four, his mother, Pat, would drive him and his younger brother, Ricky, to Candlestick Park where the two boys would play in the Giants' clubhouse while the teams were competing on the field. Barry would go from locker to locker, taking sticks of gum. He would stuff as many as he could in his mouth until he was chewing on a giant wad, just like the pros.

When Barry turned five, he got to wear a miniature Giants uniform and play on the field with his glove. He stood between his father, the Giants' rightfielder, and centerfielder Willie Mays during batting practice and shagged flies with them. Mays was one of the greatest baseball players ever. He played centerfield for the Giants most of his career. He is among the all-time leaders in runs, hits, runs batted in, and home runs. To Barry, though, Mays was just part of the family. Willie Mays is Barry's godfather.

Bobby Bonds was a great player as well. He combined power and speed to hit 30 home runs and steal 30 bases in the same season *five times*—more times than anyone in the history of the game.

At home, Barry would play pool with his father in the den. The winner would get to eat his favorite candy bar and watch the loser do push-ups. But Bobby was on the road a lot, and Barry resented it. "I really remember more about my mom," Barry says.

Willie Mays hit 660 home runs during his career. He was also a terrific outfielder and is in the baseball Hall of Fame.

"She did everything for me. She always took me to baseball or football practice. She always wrote 'from Dad' on the Christmas presents. My mom was at all the school events. My dad never went. He was playing baseball."

When Barry's father was home, he sometimes would take his son fishing on a boat in the Pacific Ocean. "I hated it," Barry says. "The minute we'd get out there, I'd get seasick. We never caught anything, and my dad would sit there and eat Oreo cookies. It was gross."

Barry seemed to prefer spending time with his mother. "I was a mama's boy. I'd rather watch my mom put on her makeup," he says, "or I would put on a wig and dance with her. We would both pretend we were Janet Jackson."

Having a superstar for a father was difficult for Barry. His baseball teammates would call him "Bobby" when he got a hit and say he was a good player only because of his father. They were jealous, of course, but Barry's feelings were hurt. He talked about it often with Dave Stephens, his baseball coach at Serra High School. Coach Stephens would comfort Barry.

If Barry was hurting inside during a game, he never showed it. Playing centerfield most of the time, Barry batted .467 in high school and led Serra High School to the Central Coast Section championship round three straight years.

Barry was an excellent baseball player at Serra High School, but he wasn't popular with his teammates.

Barry, No. 34, also played basketball and football for his high school.

Barry also played running back on the football team, and he was an all-league guard in basketball. But baseball was his first love.

Being a local hero was not easy for Barry's father. He would go to many of Barry's baseball games, but he wouldn't sit in the stands. He didn't want to steal the crowd's attention or put extra pressure on Barry. "I'd park behind some trees," Bobby remembers.

From the dugout, Barry would scan the bleachers for his father. Then he would hang his head. "My dad," Barry would whisper, "didn't come to the game." Barry never knew that his father was peering from behind a grove of trees, watching him whack the ball all over the lot.

The Serra High School baseball team was very successful with Barry as a member. He is in the back row, the fourth from the left side.

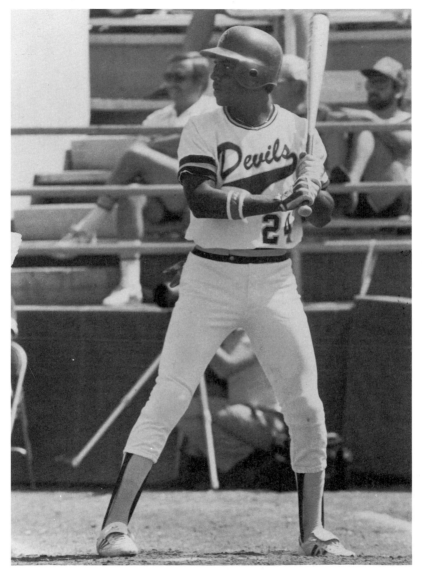

Barry played three years of college baseball for the Arizona State University Sun Devils.

3

On to the Big Leagues

Barry had always planned to go to college. Then the Giants drafted him fresh out of high school in the second round of the 1982 draft. They offered him $75,000 to sign a contract with them. Barry had a difficult decision to make. He asked his father for advice. Bobby told him to ask for $5,000 more from the Giants. Barry did. The Giants refused. Barry chose college.

Living in Tempe, Arizona, where he attended Arizona State University, was a big change for Barry. It was nothing like living in Northern California. The desert was hot and dry, and there wasn't an ocean or a beach to visit. The Arizona State baseball program was considered tops in the country, but sometimes that wasn't enough. Barry missed his home and family.

The baseball field was the one place Barry felt comfortable. Barry felt safe and sure of himself between the white lines that marked the area in play

Arizona State baseball coach Jim Brock helped Barry.

Barry played centerfield and felt comfortable there.

Jim Brock coached the Arizona State baseball team. On the field, coach Brock said, "Barry was a kid with a twinkle in his eye." Off the field, though, Barry had problems. He was moody, and some teammates even thought he was arrogant. "I had to talk to him a lot," coach Brock said. "He wanted to be liked. He tried so hard to have people like him. Tried *too* hard. He was never malicious, but he said silly things, wild statements." Barry tried to impress people so they would like him. His boasting often backfired. Some teammates ignored Barry, almost pretending he wasn't on the team.

Again, if Barry's feelings were hurt, he never showed it on the field. Playing in the College World Series as a sophomore, Barry tied an NCAA record by banging out seven straight hits as his Sun Devils nearly won the title. Barry didn't see his family much in college, but he made the most of his time there. He spent countless hours perfecting his baseball skills.

Barry understood that there was more to baseball than singles. He wanted to be a multidimensional player. The Oakland A's spring training site was nearby. A's basestealing superstar Rickey Henderson, who knew Barry's father, worked with Barry on baserunning techniques. Sun Devils batting coach Jeff Pentland taught Barry to use his strength at the plate to hit with more power. Barry responded by clubbing

23 home runs during his junior year. After that, Barry decided he was ready for pro baseball. He declared himself eligible for the 1985 major league draft.

Barry was the sixth player picked in the draft. He was chosen by the Pittsburgh Pirates. As a boy, Barry had watched Roberto Clemente, Willie Stargell, Dave Parker, and other Pirates smash baseballs out of the park. Maybe *he* would be the next Pirate bomber.

First, Barry would have to prove himself in the minor leagues. Each major league team has at least four minor league teams. The minor leagues are divided into Class AAA (the highest level), Class AA, Class A, and the rookie league. Pittsburgh sent Barry to Prince William, Virginia, to play on its team in the Class A Carolina League. There, he met another young player with plenty of potential—a big kid named Bobby Bonilla.

Barry didn't know it at the time, but he and Bonilla would become friends for life. They would hang out together, go to the movies, and share secrets. They shared something else, too. They were both on the fast track to the big leagues. They respected each other, and they teased each other, too.

One night, after Barry had struck out for the third straight time, Bonilla got all the players to throw their baseball caps on the field to honor Barry's "hat trick." Barry was angry at himself for striking out three times when he turned to go back to the dugout.

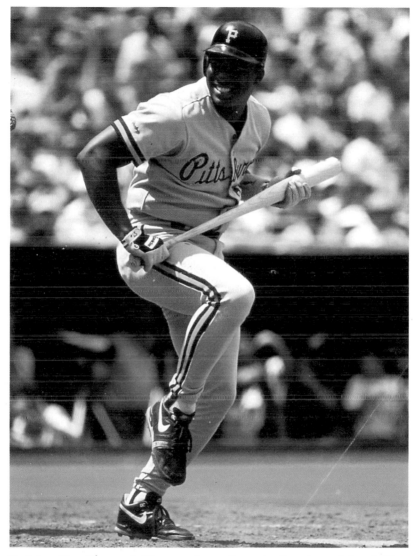

Bobby Bonilla met Barry when they both played for Pittsburgh's Class A team. Later, they were teammates on the major league Pirates.

Then he saw all the hats, and he burst out laughing. In 71 games at Prince William, he hit .299 with 13 homers and 15 stolen bases.

Barry moved up to Class AAA Hawaii for the 1986 season. But he didn't stay there long. During batting practice, before a game in Phoenix, Pirates general manager Syd Thrift saw Barry hit six balls in a row over the rightfield fence. Barry displayed great power as a pull hitter. (A lefthanded batter *pulls* the ball to rightfield.) The general manager approached Barry and said, "Any good hitter can do that. I'd like to see you hit a few over the *leftfield* fence." Thrift knew that hitting with power to the opposite field is a sign of true strength. Barry whacked five in a row over the fence in left. "Is that good enough for you?" Barry said. "That's fine," Thrift answered. Barry was taken out of the game in the fifth inning, and the general manager took him to Pittsburgh that night.

The next day, Barry was in a Pittsburgh Pirates uniform. He wore number 7 in his first year, but then he switched to number 24 because that's the number Willie Mays had worn.

In Barry's first major league game, the Los Angeles Dodgers arrived at Three Rivers Stadium to face the Pirates. Before the game, Barry checked the lineup card taped to the dugout wall. On it, he saw "Bonds CF." Barry would play centerfield and bat seventh in the lineup. He was thrilled.

Pirates general manager Syd Thrift gave Barry a chance to play in the big leagues.

That night would become even more thrilling for Barry. Against Dodgers pitcher Rick Honeycutt, Barry got his first major league hit—a double, to leftfield, the opposite field.

Five days later, while playing Atlanta, Barry hammered his first big-league home run. The New York Mets were the next team to visit Three Rivers Stadium. Slugger Darryl Strawberry stepped into the batter's box for his first at bat. At first, Strawberry didn't notice anything unusual. The Pirates appeared to be in their usual defensive alignment, with the leftfielder and rightfielder playing deep. But wait—who was the new centerfielder? And why was he standing closer to second base than the fence? Why was he playing so shallow? Nobody plays Darryl Strawberry that close. But Barry caught Darryl's blooper to center.

Barry quickly rose to the majors, but winning came later.

All Darryl could do was yell at the newcomer as he approached second base.

Afterward, Barry explained to reporters what he was doing. "I play a shallow centerfield because I believe if it stays in the park, I can run it down," Barry said. "I know there's a lot of times a Strawberry or an Eric Davis is up, and they're thinking, 'How can he play me there? Move back.' But I'm saying under my breath, 'You can't hit a ball over my head. If you think you can, prove it to me.' "

Who was this brash young rookie named Barry Bonds? Fans were quickly finding out. Even though Barry had missed the first two months of the season, he still ended up with 72 runs, 92 hits, 26 doubles, 16 homers, 48 runs batted in, and 36 stolen bases. He led all rookies in homers, RBIs and stolen bases.

Still, the Pirates finished in last place in the National League East Division. "We are not losers," Barry declared. "We may have lost, but we are not losers. We're young. We're getting better. In a year, two years, somewhere down the line, we are going to tip the city of Pittsburgh right on its ear."

Barry was asked by reporters about his performance. "I'm 22 years old and still trying to find out the type of player I am going to be in this game," he said. "But I'm not so concerned about my own individual self as I am about my team winning."

That was about to happen.

4

Never Quite Enough

Barry had reached the big leagues fast. He could hardly believe he was a pro when he showed up for spring training to start his second year. Here he was, playing against boyhood heroes like Ozzie Smith, Dave Winfield, and Mike Schmidt.

Barry was absolutely in awe the day he faced all-time great pitcher Nolan Ryan. Barry was so over-whelmed he struck out three times in a row, on three pitches every time. One-two-three. One-two-three. One-two-three. Bobby Bonds had told his son to just relax and pretend he was playing in high school. "Are you kidding?" Barry said. "This is Nolan Ryan!"

Still, Barry certainly was focused in the regular season. When the Pirates acquired centerfielder Andy Van Slyke a month into the season, Barry was switched to leftfield. He batted leadoff, scored 99 runs, stole 32 bases, and clubbed 25 home runs. It was a great season.

Bobby Bonds' excellent major league career was hard for Barry to match.

To some, however, Barry hadn't done enough. Barry's father had his first 30-30 season (at least 30 home runs and 30 stolen bases) in his second year. People wondered why Barry couldn't do what his father did. Bobby had retired from baseball the year Barry went to college.

Barry didn't like being compared to his father, but he would only say, "I don't have his strength." Pirates general manager Syd Thrift was more direct. "I'm sure at times," Thrift said, "he wishes he had a different last name." Bobby kept quiet about the issue, not wishing to upset his son. Besides, there was little he could say.

The 1988 season was even better. The fall before, Barry had met a young Swedish woman. Barry and Sun, short for Susann, fell in love and were married on February 6, 1988.

When the season began, Barry was ready to play. In Pittsburgh's first 12 games, he had seven doubles, two triples, five homers, and a .365 batting average. Halfway through the year, he was leading the league in runs scored and home runs when manager Jim Leyland gave him a day off. Barry had a sore knee, and he was pleased to get a day of rest. He was on the bench in the eighth inning with the Pirates and Giants locked in a 3-3 tie. Suddenly, Barry was summoned as a pinch hitter. He unwrapped a bandage from around his sore knee, walked to the plate, and smacked Joe Price's first pitch over the centerfield wall to win the game.

Barry's biggest thrill came late in the season against Philadelphia. First, he watched his father play in an old-timers game and conk a home run. Then Barry rapped out four hits, including a home run, to lead the Pirates to a 10-4 victory over the Phillies. "Having my father there is an inspiration to me," Barry said, smiling. "Maybe I should have him travel with me."

But the Pirates missed the playoffs—again. Barry couldn't get used to losing. Unfortunately, the losing continued the following season.

In one 1989 game at Philadelphia, Barry batted first and drilled a home run. The Pirates scored 10 runs in the first inning. But, in an example of the way the 1989 season went, Pittsburgh lost the game. Barry's homer tied a major league record for most home runs in careers by a father-son combination. But what good were personal achievements, Barry wondered, if the team wasn't winning?

Barry broke the father-son record a few weeks later when he socked a pinch-hit, three-run homer off San Francisco pitcher Steve Bedrosian. The record had been 407 combined homers, held by Yogi and Dale Berra and by Gus and Buddy Bell.

Still, the Pirates wound up being the only team in their division not to make the playoffs during the decade of the '80s. Barry was extremely frustrated. He expected more from his friend Bobby Bonilla and the rest of his teammates. Beyond that, he expected more out of himself.

Then, all at once, the fortunes of Barry Bonds and the Pittsburgh Pirates changed. It happened in a barbershop. Barry explains it this way: "I went to get a haircut. This was in the off-season, in 1989, at Fred Tate's barbershop in Pittsburgh. I'm getting my hair cut, and they have the radio on.

Losing left Barry frustrated and disappointed.

"A guy on the radio says what a great athlete Randall Cunningham is, but what a great *quarterback* Joe Montana is. I weighed the two and thought, I'm so bored with having great *ability*. I want to be a great *player* like Joe Montana. So that haircut was my inspiration. I realized that what I'd been doing—cutting myself short—was wrong. Wrong to me, my team, and even the game. That's when I thought, I'm going to work my tail end off before it becomes too late."

Barry hit the weights. He jogged. He spent hours at a time in the batting cage. He trained alone five days a week, five hours a day. "We'd start working out at 10:30 in the morning," Pirates strength coach Warren Sipp said. "Every day, Barry would be in the parking lot, waiting for me."

Barry showed up for the 1990 season a changed man. He wore a gold-studded earring in his left ear and two-tone "Say No To Drugs" wristbands. He displayed a showy quick-wristed snap catch in leftfield, flicking down his glove when he snared the ball. He moved to fifth in the batting order to drive in more runs. And he clobbered the ball like never before.

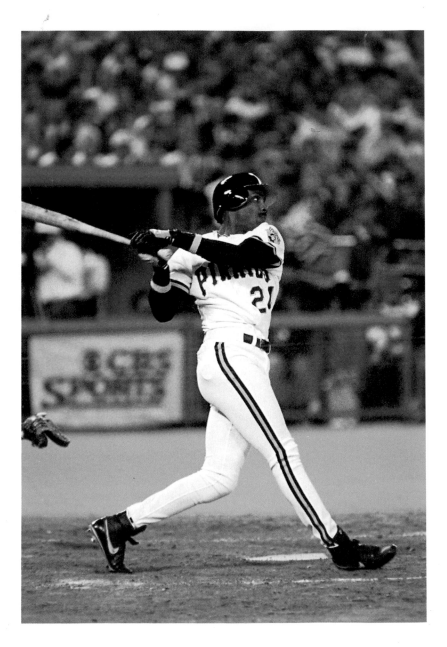

The season didn't start out very well. Barry had decided that he would get at least one hit in every game. When he didn't get a hit in the second game of the season, he was furious. "I was mad the whole week," he said. "The *whole week*. I was mad because I blew my streak."

Barry didn't let his anger disrupt his concentration at the plate. He jumped out to a hot streak and stayed hot all summer. He became the talk of Pittsburgh.

"When it comes to ability, Barry's the greatest player I've ever played with, or will ever play with," centerfielder Andy Van Slyke said. "I think one day he will put up numbers that no one can believe," rightfielder R.J. Reynolds said. "He's what this franchise was waiting for," third baseman Bobby Bonilla said.

Barry was polite to his teammates, but he didn't care much for reporters. Sometimes he told them so. Reporters wrote that Barry was "a bad guy to have in the clubhouse." Whispers circulated about Barry's arrogant attitude.

Barry's agent, Rod Wright, defended Barry by saying, "Barry puts up a front because he doesn't want people to know who he is." Manager Leyland also came to Barry's defense, saying, "Barry Bonds plays hard, and he plays hurt. I'm satisfied."

Barry was a terror at the plate. He batted .301 that year with 33 home runs, 114 RBIs and 52 stolen bases. He won a Gold Glove award for his fielding.

Pittsburgh manager Jim Leyland supported Barry and defended him when others were critical of his effort.

Baseball writers selected him as the National League Most Valuable Player. "I'm shocked," Barry said. "My rapport with reporters isn't good." Best of all, the Pirates finally made the playoffs.

In the National League Championship Series against the Cincinnati Reds, the heart of the Pittsburgh lineup fell into a slump. Van Slyke, Bonilla, and Bonds, the three-four-five hitters, batted just .190

with five RBIs in six games. The Reds beat the Pirates and advanced to the World Series, where they swept the Oakland A's to win the title.

Barry's hard work had turned the Pirates into contenders. He led them to another division title in 1991. But again, his bat fell silent in the playoffs. Pittsburgh led the Atlanta Braves three games to two in the National League Championship Series. The Pirates needed just one more victory to reach the World Series. But they lost Game 6 and Game 7 at Three Rivers, and the Braves advanced to the championship. Barry hit just .148 without an RBI in the seven games. Atlanta third baseman Terry Pendleton edged Barry in the league MVP voting.

Then Barry heard the worst news of all. Barry's best friend, Bobby Bonilla, left the Pirates to sign with the New York Mets. Barry cried for days. Then he thought maybe it was time for him to go, too. He had one year left on his contract. Then he would become a free agent and could receive offers from any club that wanted him. Every team wanted Barry. He knew for sure that the 1992 season would be his last with Pittsburgh when team officials told him at spring training, "You're just too expensive for us."

Still, Barry was happy at home. Sun had given birth to a baby boy. Barry and Sun named him Nikolai.

Barry stayed focused on the baseball field. He batted .311 with 34 home runs. He had 39 stolen bases.

New York Mets general manager Al Harazin, left, Bobby Bonilla, and Mets manager Jeff Torborg celebrate Bonilla's joining the Mets with Bonilla's three-year-old daughter.

He won another Gold Glove and league Most Valuable Player award. He appeared as a guest on television programs like *Late Night with David Letterman* and *The Tonight Show*. He was simply the best player in baseball.

For the third straight year, Barry led the Pirates to the playoffs. Once again, though, disaster struck for the Pirates. It was as if Barry's team were cursed in the playoffs. The Pirates led the Atlanta Braves, 2-0, in the ninth inning of the decisive seventh game. Pittsburgh was one inning away from making it to the 1992 World Series. Thousands of fans at Atlanta-Fulton County Stadium stood with their fingers crossed. Millions of people were watching on television.

Barry and Andy Van Slyke, right, were two of Pittsburgh's top players in the 1992 playoffs.

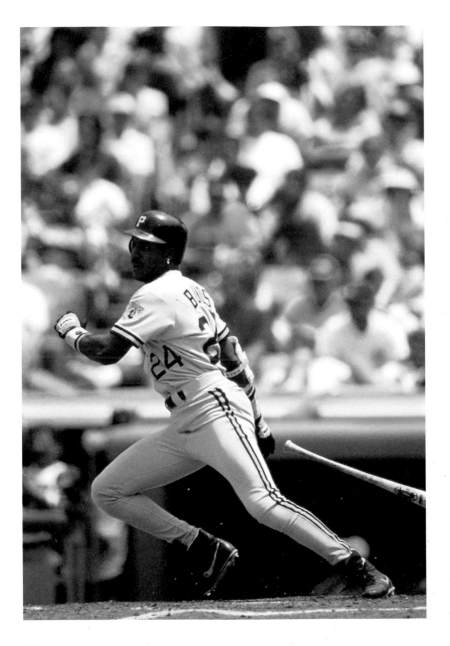

The Braves rallied. They scored a run. The bases were loaded with two outs. The Pirates still led, 2-1. A little-known player, Francisco Cabrera, was sent in to pinch hit. Barry stood anxiously in leftfield. One more out was all the Pirates needed. *One more out.*

Barry imagined a strikeout and then rushing in to celebrate with his teammates. It didn't happen. Cabrera lined a single to left. Barry moved to his right and charged the ball. Dave Justice scored for the Braves to tie the game, and Sid Bream was rounding third with the winning run. Barry gloved the ball quickly and threw hard to the plate. Catcher Mike LaValliere snared the perfect throw. Bream slid. LaValliere tagged him. Umpire Randy Marsh made the call. *Safe!*

Jubilant Atlanta fans poured onto the field. The Braves mobbed Bream at home plate. Barry slumped to the ground and sat motionless. He was stunned. Just like that, it was over. His season—his *career*—with the Pirates was over.

Willie Mays, left, Bobby Bonds, center, and Barry were re-
united in 1993 when Barry joined the Giants.

5

A Giant Star

After leaving Pittsburgh, Barry wanted to play for a team in California. There were five—the San Diego Padres, the Los Angeles Dodgers, the California Angels, the Oakland A's, and the Giants. Barry told reporters, "I want to play for any California team except the Giants because it's cold in San Francisco and they need a new stadium." Barry's childhood dream of playing for the Giants had been replaced by a dose of reality. Candlestick Park was well known for chilly winds blowing off the San Francisco Bay, even in the summer. Outfielders had a difficult time trying to catch windblown balls. It was not a fun place to play.

Giants owner Peter Magowan called Barry anyway. He said Barry belonged in San Francisco and that he would pay him a lot of money to join the team. He didn't say how much, just a lot of money. Barry thought about the money, about his father, about shagging flies in the outfield as a boy, about coming home. He agreed to join the Giants.

A few minutes later, the telephone rang again. It was Barry's agent. "Barry Bonds," his agent said excitedly, "this is your contract." Barry listened to the numbers. He almost fell to the floor. "My head blew up like a balloon," Barry said. "I wanted to go to the Empire State Building and jump, since I could fly at that point. Then I got nervous. Scared." A thousand thoughts and feelings flooded through Barry. The deal was this: six years, $44 million. *Forty-four million dollars!*

The Giants held a press conference to introduce their new leftfielder, who was the highest-paid player

In 1993, Giants owner Peter Magowan decided to pay Barry the biggest salary in baseball.

Barry and his wife Sun celebrate Barry's decision to sign with the San Francisco Giants.

in all of sports. Reporters asked Barry what it felt like to come home. Emotions gripped him again, and Barry began to cry as he spoke. "Will Clark, Matt Williams, Robby Thompson, they're all determined to win," he said. "I have never been more excited to play in a city in my entire life than I am now."

The Giants had finished 26 games behind in the standings the previous year. But the 1993 season felt

51

like a brand-new start for Bay Area baseball fans. The new manager was Dusty Baker. The new leftfielder was a superstar. The new batting coach was Bobby Bonds. Everything seemed perfect for Barry. Barry's wife, Sun, had given birth to their second child, a daughter they named Shikari.

Barry took the field for the home opener at Candlestick Park wearing number 25—his father's old number. A large banner with the words "The Bonds Squad" hung over the railing in the leftfield bleachers. For his first at bat as a San Francisco Giant, Barry hit a fastball high over "The Bonds Squad" sign for a home run.

Bobby, left, became the San Francisco batting coach when Barry signed with the team.

Bobby helped Barry work on his swing.

The stadium shook with applause. It was the beginning of a great season for Barry and the Giants.

Barry also endeared himself to San Francisco fans by buying $10,000 worth of tickets and giving them to children during the summer months. He gave away 50 tickets for each of 42 games. The kids sat in left-field above "The Bonds Squad" sign. When he took the field in the first inning, Barry would always look up to the stands and tip his cap to the children.

By the end of the 1993 season, the Giants were racing the Braves for the playoffs. They had the two best records in baseball. Barry wanted his new team to make it to the postseason. His desire boosted his

Willie Mays presented Barry with the 1992 MVP award, his second of four awards.

playing with exciting results. Needing a victory in a close game against the Cubs, Barry and Matt Williams slugged back-to-back homers twice in one game. In the final 16 games of the season, Barry almost single-handedly carried the team with six homers, seven doubles, 21 RBIs, and a slugging percentage of .660.

He was the most feared hitter in baseball because he led the league in home runs, runs batted in, and slugging percentage. He could run, throw, field, hit for average, and hit for power—the five things that measure a player's ability.

The Giants were one game behind the Braves on the last day of the season when they met the Dodgers in Los Angeles. Scoreless until the third inning, the Dodgers broke through with two runs. They scored again in the fourth, but the Giants scored in the fifth inning to make it 3-1. Then the Dodgers exploded. They won the game 12-1.

It was a crushing end to San Francisco's promising year. Barry had posted amazing numbers: .331 average, 46 home runs, 123 RBIs, 29 stolen bases. He was an easy choice again as the league's Most Valuable Player, his third MVP award. Still, Barry was not satisfied. He yearned to play in the World Series.

In 1994 he missed out again. With two months left of the season, Barry already had 37 home runs, 81 RBIs, and 29 stolen bases. The Giants were three games behind the Dodgers in the standings, but closing fast. Then it all stopped.

The players went on strike. Baseball players and owners couldn't agree on salaries. Barry was paid well, but he supported his teammates. The issue wasn't resolved, and the season came to a halt. For the first time since 1904, there was no World Series.

Barry was also having a bad time at home. He and Sun had decided to get a divorce. Although they would no longer live together, they agreed to share the care of their two children.

The 1995 season was much better for Barry. The Giants started slowly, but Barry brought them back with his power. When Giants cleanup hitter Matt Williams suffered a broken foot, Barry tried to carry the offense by himself, but he couldn't do it. Opposing pitchers frustrated Barry by not giving him many good pitches to hit. Barry wound up leading the league with 120 walks.

When Barry did hit the ball, he usually hit it with power. He finished with 33 home runs and 31 stolen bases. It was the third time he had achieved the 30-30 mark. Unfortunately, the Giants finished the 1995 season in last place by 11 games.

The following year wasn't much better for the Giants.

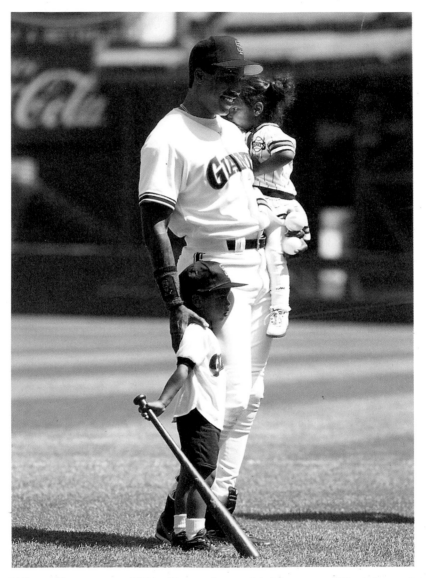

When they were little, Barry brought his son, Nikolai, and his daughter, Shikari, to the ballpark.

They lost 94 times, firmly putting the team in last place. Although Barry's efforts didn't boost the team out of its rut, they did gain him entrance into two prestigious clubs. Barry joined his father, Willie Mays, and Andre Dawson as the only players to achieve 300 home runs and 300 stolen bases in their careers. Barry also became just the second person to tally a 40-40 season.

After two years in last place, the Giants made a change. Team managers traded the veteran Matt Williams for four talented young players. At the start of the 1997 season, the Giants charged into first place. The Dodgers soon joined the race. These two California clubs fought each other for first place the rest of the season.

When they met for a doubleheader in September, the Dodgers had a two-game lead. In the first inning of the first game, Barry smacked a two-run homer into the upper deck to drive in both runs of a 2-1 win. Barry proved even more helpful in the second game of the set. He hit a triple and scored on Glenallen Hill's single. Then in the fifth inning he whacked a three-run homer into the bleachers. Barry was the first player to rush onto the field in celebration when the Giants finally won the game in the twelfth inning.

The Giants went on to earn their first postseason appearance in eight years. But they lost the Division

Series against the Florida Marlins, who ended up capturing the 1997 World Championship title. The Giants couldn't feel too bad; they'd turned a losing team into a winning team in just one season.

For Barry, life was getting better and better. He pulled off his fifth 30-30 season in 1997, matching his father for the most 30-30 seasons in National League history. Then, in January of 1998, Barry married Liz Watson. (The couple had a daughter, Aisha, about one year later.) Barry earned his eighth All-Star selection. The 1998 season ended with the Giants just missing their second consecutive postseason appearance.

Barry produced another outstanding season in 1999, despite missing numerous games due to injuries. Problems with his left elbow, groin, and knee allowed Barry to play only 102 games, a career low. With the Giants out of contention, attention focused on enjoying Candlestick Park's last season. In the farewell ceremony, Giants great Willie Mays threw Barry the stadium's last pitch before home plate was removed and transported by helicopter to its new home, Pacific Bell Park.

The first season in the new park sold out. Nearly 3.3 million fans gathered to watch San Francisco win their second division title in 4 years. Barry liked testing the limits of the new stadium. He hit a career-high 49 home runs that season, many reaching the water behind the rightfield wall at Pacific Bell Park.

Fans crowded into McCovey Cove behind Pacific Bell Park, hoping to grab Barry's 70th home run.

Then came 2001. Barry broke records. He made new fans. His teammates noticed that he smiled more. Before long, against the Dodgers, Barry raised the record to 73 home runs. "To be able to say I wanted to do something in my heart and [actually do] it was really, really meaningful," explained Barry. People all over the country took notice. Barry had indeed accomplished something special.

But that's not all he did. For posting amazing numbers and phenomenal records, Barry received the MVP award for the fourth time in his career—more times than anyone in the history of baseball. "It boils down to true love and passion for the game," Giants manager Dusty Baker said. "Money and records can only motivate you so far." At 37 years old, Barry produced another great season in a career of great seasons. In January of 2002, Barry signed a 5-year contract with the Giants. After another impressive season in 2002, the future continues to shine brightly for the man whose potential and accomplishments often appear larger than life.